Elephant Painter

by Janet Buell

Scott Foresman

Editorial Offices: Glenview, Illinois • New York, New York
Sales Offices: Reading, Massachusetts • Duluth, Georgia
Glenview, Illinois • Carrollton, Texas • Menlo Park, California

Mary is an animal artist. No, she doesn't paint deer. She doesn't paint ducks or wolves. Mary is an animal.

She is an Asian elephant.

Mary lives at the Riddle Elephant Sanctuary in Arkansas. This is a home for unwanted elephants. She lives with Heidi and Scott Riddle and their three children.

Long ago, Mary was a circus elephant. Then her owners sold the circus. Her new owners had a hard time with Mary. She wouldn't do some things they wanted. The new owners didn't want to keep Mary. They sold her to the Riddles. The Riddles have nine other elephants besides Mary.

The Riddles love all their elephants. They train them. They care for them. They want their elephants to be happy.

Some elephants use sticks to draw in the dirt. Some like to stack rocks.

Mary liked to hold a stick in her trunk. She doodled in the dirt with the stick. That inspired the Riddles to try something. They thought Mary might like to paint.

**The end of an elephant's trunk
is called a "finger."**

Mary has a short trunk for an elephant. It is
a useful trunk. She uses it to do many things. She
learned these things in the circus. She can ring
a bell. She can beat a drum. She can shake a rattle.
The Riddles thought Mary could learn to hold
a brush.

The Riddles gave Mary her first art lesson. They put a canvas in front of her. Many artists paint on canvas. A canvas is a piece of thick cloth. The cloth is stretched over a wood frame. The canvas doesn't have a border like some pictures. A framed border comes after the picture is done.

The Riddles showed Mary how to use a brush. At first, Mary didn't understand. She smashed the brush at the canvas. She punched a hole in it. Some of the bristles came off. They stuck on the canvas. It was quite a messy scene!

The Riddles showed Mary again and again. After a week or two, she could use her brush the right way.

After many years, Mary's paintings are much better. At first she just slapped paint on the canvas. Now she paints carefully.

The Riddles sell Mary's paintings. They use the money to buy food for their elephants. People as far away as London and New York buy Mary's paintings. Some of them sell for $250!

Some people say Mary makes abstract paintings. An abstract painting may not show the kind of scene we know. It may just show wavy lines. It may be a jumble of colors. When you look at an abstract painting, you might see a scene with trees and blowing leaves. Someone else might look at the same picture. He might see laundry spinning in a dryer!

This is an abstract painting by Wassily Kandinsky.

Mary painted these.

Some people say Mary isn't really an artist. They say only people are inspired to show the world and their feelings. They believe elephants paint only to get a treat.

Is Mary an inspired artist?

When he was four years old, Briac Riddle painted with Mary.

Like all elephants, Mary is smart. She seems to know what she likes. She doesn't like very light colors. She doesn't like very dark colors, either. She chooses bright colors every time.

Sometimes Mary paints on only one part of the canvas. The Riddles try hard to get her to paint on the other parts. Mary won't.

Some days Mary likes to use big brushes. Some days she likes little brushes. Mary knows what her brushes can do. When she uses big brushes, she uses big strokes. When she uses little brushes, she uses little strokes.

Mary holds up her foot when she is done. She shakes her head no. Some days, Mary paints many pictures. Some days she doesn't like to paint at all. On those days she shakes her head no when she sees her brushes.

Mary isn't the only elephant that paints. There are several other elephants that paint too.

This painting was made by Ruby, an elephant at the Phoenix Zoo.

Elephants can't talk. We don't know how they feel about painting. What do you think?
Can elephants be inspired artists?